Rapid Cost Reduction & Problem Resolution

Practical Handbook for Maximum Cost
Reduction & Chronic Problem Resolution

Paul Jones

Table of Contents

Note: The views and opinions expressed in this publication represent the views of the author only and do not represent the views of any other individual, company or organization.

Foreword

Billions of dollars of unrealized savings are hidden in non-optimized products and chronic, unresolved problems.

This book is designed to share effective processes for cost reduction and problem resolution but more importantly to share the critical implementation methodologies which differentiates time and again between savings realization and traditional process failure.

Leveraging years of consulting, actual process facilitation and successful project experience, learn the secrets to effective cost reduction and rapid chronic problem resolution irrespective of industry or product type.

Section A - Product Cost Reduction

Chapter 1 – Introduction – Cost Reduction

The content of this book is based on successful cost reduction project experience not theories or hypotheses. Having observed companies large and small struggle to efficiently run cost reduction programs I felt compelled to create this book and share simple, proven methodologies that have and continue to yield significant savings irrespective of industry or product type.

Effective cost reduction is difficult, not necessarily in concept but process implementation and actual savings realization. Product cost remains one of the critical attributes in determining the commercial success of a product yet rarely gets the attention it deserves at the appropriate point in the product development process.

This book is based on years of accrued experience facilitating cost reduction projects while consulting on-site at various global companies from small start-ups to large OEMs at various stages in the product development process. The objective is to share the methodology that continually yielded success but more importantly share critical process lessons learned to enable your organization to maximize savings with minimal investment of both time, money and resources. Cost reduction ideas are worthless unless they are implemented.

The methodology presented is not designed to aggressively erode supplier margins or compromise product quality. On the contrary, this approach is designed to provide mutual benefit to both the product owner and the supply base in an effort to establish a collaborative, long term profitable relationship where everyone benefits and is willing to actively participate in this creative and mutually beneficial product optimization and cost reduction process.

The primary objective of this section is to assist in product cost reduction, however, the secondary objective is to help enable a catalytic effect in transforming the organizational perspective on cost and improve the integration of cost reduction from concept development through to production and beyond for existing and future products.

This section of the book is structured with an initial focus on high-level process lessons learned in an effort to share common pitfalls and associated mitigation strategies. It then evolves to the cost workshop forum, opportunity validation followed by ultimately the implementation and actual savings realization.

Chapter 2 - Cost Reduction Lessons Learned

Whether participating in design, product validation or cost reduction activities, one of the most valuable continuous improvement initiatives a company can promote is the capturing and publication of lessons learned. It is important to continually reference this database to ensure historic product cost inefficiencies are not repeated and that both products and processes continue to evolve and improve to reduce costs. This is especially true for organizations with high staff turn-over.

Documented in this chapter are proven cost reduction lessons learned accumulated over many years of cost reduction program facilitation which have been instrumental in consistently yielding positive results. These are presented at the beginning to allow the reader to consider their process and organizational integration as the methodology is further described.

Cost Reduction Lessons Learned

Dedicated Cost Management Resources: To maximize the productivity of any cost reduction initiative, companies must be prepared to dedicate an independent resource to facilitate the process and take primary responsibility for driving and achieving results. Traditionally, cost reduction initiatives tend to be intermittent and peripheral activities, the intensity of which highly dependent on resource availability. Cost Reduction programs often lack champions with clearly defined and realistically achievable targets. Typically, a shared responsibility amongst various organizations (primarily engineering and supply chain), cost reduction initiatives often lack rigor as more tangible and pressing day to day activities take resource priority. In addition, there can also be the cultural reluctance to identify opportunities due to the potential additional spin-off work associated with implementation.

Cost reduction programs are relatively unique in that they drive disruption to the status-quo in the form of cost driven product changes. It requires strong, independent leadership capable of good cross-functional communication to drive an opportunity to full realization. Identifying cost reduction as an independent function or group within an organization can be instrumental in achieving positive results. Appointing a high-caliber individual with well rounded technical and commercial experience to fill this position of cost manager is key.

Steering Committee: Cost reduction initiatives require more senior level guidance and monitoring than more traditional product development activities. This is primarily due to the ambiguity and uncertainty associated with opportunities and the ease at which these can be nullified and associated potential savings lost. In addition, many cost reduction initiatives can require significant investment. This requirement alone can lead to the demise of many great ideas unless an experienced third part decision maker is actively analyzing value propositions and associated Return On Investments (ROI).

The participation of a steering committee (2-3 people with the appropriate technical experience and commercial decision-making power) can be instrumental in driving the process forward. The principal roles of the steering committee include driving consensus on opportunity prioritization, roadblock removal, investment authorization and driving results to a specific timeline. A weekly report from the Cost Manager providing insight into project status, roadblocks, data gaps and resource needs can be instrumental in rapidly driving the process forward.

Cultural Alignment, Embracing Change: Cost reduction programs tend to meet resistance as they are synonymous with creating disruptions into the product development environment in the form of unplanned product changes. Engineers are typically opposed to non-functional related changes, especially cost driven ones.

Aligning organizations with the goals of the process and developing a willingness to embrace new ideas is critical to maximizing the process effectiveness. The "not-invented-here" attitude is a typical example of the type of resistance one can encounter often preventing the implementation of low risk, high value ideas.

It is relatively easy to find reasons not to implement a new idea; it is traditionally more culturally challenging for an engineering organization to accept and embrace an external concept which may be an improvement over the existing design and drive it to completion. Communicating the fundamental commercial need for cost reduction can help the cultural transition in most organizations and make it a more palatable, accepted and routine practice. Incentivizing cost improvement programs can also drive dramatic results.

Requirements & Specifications: Incorrect or misinterpreted requirements can drive excessive product costs at the various product development stages from concept development through to design commercialization and procurement.

Product requirements are defined by the target market and the final customer of the product or service. These requirements are usually captured by the sales and marketing teams through extensive market due-diligence using quality function deployment methodologies such as peer review groups and competitive product analysis such as benchmarking.

Engineering specifications are generated by engineers to ensure that a product meets these customer requirements at various ends of a tolerance envelope. Engineering specifications that overshoot the requirements can result in a higher than required product content, higher subsequent costs which can result in reduced margins. Specifications undershooting the requirements can result in lost sales and customer dissatisfaction due to misalignment with customer needs. Ironically, requirements often receive less scrutiny than specifications but are the principal drivers of product specifications, costs and subsequent margins.

If Specifications > Requirements = Lost Potential Savings

A hidden way in which companies unknowingly drive excessive costs can occur during the sharing of technical information with suppliers. Over constraining suppliers can lead to excessive costs and risks. Allowing suppliers the freedom to interpret requirements and develop optimized specifications which align with their equipment and processes can lead to cost reduction opportunities without compromising their margins.

Opportunities include but are not limited to:

- Allowing the supplier to leverage economies of scale with other products for other customers

- Enabling greater flexibility to use existing equipment avoiding the procurement of new equipment and/or set-up fees

- Not dictating manufacturing processes to suppliers. If the dimensions of the final part are what really matter, don't over constrain the supplier

The Power of "Should Cost" Analysis Tools: This powerful, underutilized cost analysis toolset generates the true cost of a component or sub-system by forensic analysis of materials and processes used to manufacture it. By developing granular cost insight into materials and processes it is possible to accurately determine the true manufacturing cost models of most components irrespective of complexity, material content, size, production location and volume.

When used and applied correctly, this remains one of the most powerful Design for Cost (DFC) and Design for Manufacture (DFM) tools an organization can apply to understand and drive down the design and manufacturing costs of any component and/or system. It is especially powerful during the concept development stage where designs and material selection is still flexible.

The level of granularity that this analysis provides is invaluable at all phases of the product development cycle but can be especially useful during the procurement process as a powerful negotiation tool because of the transparency it provides.

Numerous consulting companies provide "should-cost" analysis services. Leveraging these external resources reduces the knowledge ramp-up time and minimizes internal overhead expertise requirements (especially in smaller organizations). Typically, these consulting organizations use active databases of materials, manufacturing equipment, critical process parameters all linked to a dynamic cost model providing in many cases more cost granularity and accuracy than the suppliers developing and producing the actual product.

The principal differentiator that ultimately defines the quality of the data produced is the expertise of the manufacturing team applying the analysis tools and generating the data. Interviewing the team of consultants and familiarizing oneself with their specific experience prior to engaging is highly recommended. Typically, these organizations have dedicated casting, stamping, materials and electrical component experts on staff. Providing accurate process information prior to the analysis maximizes the output accuracy.

Typical cost models include the following elements:

- Engineering (Design & Validation Costs)
- Capital Investment & Amortization Strategies
- Material Assumptions
- Manufacturing Labor Cost & Cycle Times
- Quality
- Tooling
- SG&A
- Profit Margin
- Logistics
- Energy Usage and Cost

In addition to the traditional elements of a cost model, one should also consider the following total cost of ownership elements such as warranty costs.

There are multiple ways to use "should-cost" data generated to reduce product costs:

- **Design for Cost (DFC):** During the product development and product evolution/upgrade stages by directing the selection of materials and features to minimize costs through design optimization.

- **Design for Manufacturing (DFM):** Enabling the selection of optimum processes to minimize manufacturing process costs through the development of cost models. Insight into how tolerances drive cost in various components can assist in complex tolerance distribution and optimization exercises.

- **Attribute Trade-Off Analysis:** Investigating various design permutations and evaluating attribute trade-offs as they relate to cost.

- **Outsourcing Strategy Development:** Optimizing a product sourcing strategy using derived data to drive decisions and manage risks. These cost analysis toolsets allow the selection of various markets, adjusting labor rates, local machining and logistic costs.

- **Competitive Cost Benchmarking:** Generating competitive benchmark data by evaluating the true cost of competitor products and associated manufacturing methodologies.

- **Cost Curve Generation:** Accurately predicting the effects of volume on costs can be difficult without "should-cost" analysis methods. Once complete, they can be overlaid with the supplier curves for gap comparison.

- **Supplier Interaction:** Presenting prepared data to a supplier as a reference in the negotiation process in an effort to reconcile the cost/price gap. This tool can also be used collaboratively to assist suppliers in the optimization of their manufacturing and procurement strategy.

Early Price and Cost Reconciliation: Many organizations share the common deficiency of embarking on a new product commercialization activity without a thorough understanding of the actual price the target market is prepared to pay.

Generation of cost curves at the beginning of a program and continuous evolution of these curves throughout the product development process can be instrumental in ensuring that the product is correctly aligned with the market price tolerance reducing the risk of post launch re-design efforts.

Cost as a Key Functional Requirement: A common occurrence in product development is the dismissal of cost as a critical product attribute until late in the product development process. This can force late and sometimes major re-design efforts driven by these cost gaps.

An effective method of preventing this problem is the inclusion of cost as a key functional requirement within engineering documentation such as concept FMEAs and design FMEAs where the risk of not meeting the functional requirements can be evaluated, a validation plan established and countermeasures generated at the appropriate time prior to making significant investment in tooling and validation.

Cost Transparency: Most Supply Chain personnel cringe when the phrase "open-book-pricing" or "cost transparency" is mentioned in the context of suppliers and procurement. There is a general perception that it can violate the privacy of a supplier and their proprietary processes. It is also expected that conversations on the subject could be met with strong resistance.

Having exposure to the principal cost drivers in any product is fundamental for the engineering and cost management teams to ensure that both the engineering and sourcing teams are focused on addressing the cost drivers as the product is developed. It is generally assumed that suppliers will not provide "open-book-pricing", however, the reality can be very different. It never hurts to ask and the rewards can be mutually beneficial if managed correctly.

Cost & Price, Multiple Quotes: The cost of a product is what it actually costs a supplier to make, the price is what the market is prepared to pay (cost + applied margin). There is little relationship between cost and price. Submitting five request for quotes (RFQs) when sourcing doesn't mean the lowest quote received is the best achievable. Having insight into actual costs using "should-cost" toolsets can be invaluable when negotiating final price.

Mandatory Cost Curves: Every component should have an associated cost curve. Access to cost curves allows the organization to project product cost, plan future pricing strategies, optimize volumes but more importantly manage margin expectations. By overlaying sub-component cost curves, companies can understand critical break points in an effort to optimize raw material procurement strategies. More importantly, cost curves can provide early warning on products that require significant cost reduction attention.

Cost Curve Example

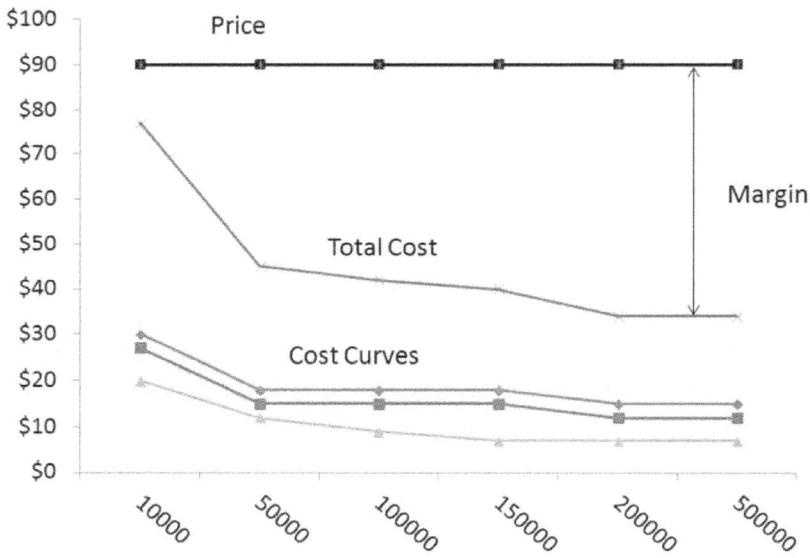

When to Engage Consultants: Leveraging consultants is a useful way to supplement an organization skillset with expertise and experience without the cost burden of a partially used, full time resource. There are numerous ways in which consultants can support cost reduction projects:

- **Process Facilitation:** Cost reduction process facilitation. Having a non-employee facilitate the process can be instrumental in driving objectivity

- **Technical Consulting:** DFC & DFM

- **Cost Model Generation:** Supporting cost model generation through application of should cost analysis methodologies. Without transparency of the cost drivers, it is impossible to develop opportunities.

Chapter 3 - The Cost Reduction Workshop

The cost reduction workshop is the most important step in the process of identifying savings opportunities.

Effective facilitation of this workshop transforms a generic value engineering activity into a focused, objective, data driven process with quantifiable targets and actionable projects that produce realizable savings. More importantly, it enables capturing of ideas from a large population of cross-functional thinkers who would not otherwise be engaged or be able to contribute to the product development process.

This workshop is the platform for idea generation, classification, prioritization and most importantly developing a plan for implementation and savings realization. Prior to launching the workshop, it is important to have a process owner who thoroughly understands and embraces the process methodology and is both willing and capable of educating and motivating the workshop participants.

Multi-Step Cost Reduction Workshop Process

Step 1 - Establishing Credible Cost Targets

Highlighting the gap between current and target system costs is key to conditioning the participants in any cost workshop environment. Presenting a cost target too high can limit the opportunities whereas an overly ambitious cost target can lose credibility and de-motivate the team prior to process even starting. The target cost should be data driven and can be developed using a combination of sources such as business model requirements and competitive product benchmarking data.

Remember, benchmarking competitor products only represents current production and not what is potentially in their pipeline for future release. This must be factored into all competitive cost evaluations in an effort to develop realistic goals.

Step 2 - Providing Current Product Cost Insight

It is important to calibrate workshop participants on existing component costs to enable them to understand the baseline and principle cost drivers of the product being targeted. More importantly, this information helps improve the accuracy of estimating incremental savings for any ideas generated.

Suggested Workshop Activities:

- **Publication of Costed BOM:** Publishing a costed BOM prior to the workshop provides participants necessary insight into all sub-components and their respective costs. In addition, separating tooling, machining and logistic costs is also useful as these can be significant contributors and targets for cost reduction. Displaying a costed BOM at the actual cost workshop can be especially useful as a quick reference for participants as they examine each sub-system and component.

- **Publication of Cost Pareto:** Understanding the cost distribution in a product allows the team to understand the principal cost drivers of the assembled product but more importantly which components to focus on. Clearly, spending 90% of one's time on 5% of the product cost drivers doesn't make sense.

Step 2 Workshop Output Products:

1. *Excel File with BOM and associated costs for each component*

2. *Pareto Illustrating cost distribution (relative percentage)*

Step 3 - Reconciling Requirements & Specifications

When requesting that participants generate cost reduction ideas it is important that they review and understand the product requirements, not just the engineering specifications. One must never forget that product specifications are the engineering team's interpretation of what is needed to meet the requirements.

An alternative, lower cost product specification which achieves the same performance requirements while generating cost savings is always preferable assuming that any differences are transparent to the end customer.

Exceeding customer requirements adds unnecessary cost and fails to provide customers additional value. With access to advanced materials technologies, predictive analysis toolsets, instrumentation to analyze duty cycles and advanced testing methodologies, there is no justifiable reason to have a design that is not optimized to align with the market/customer requirements and strictly nothing more.

Before embarking on reconciling a design to a set of requirements, it is a prudent exercise to confirm that the requirements as documented align with both current and future market needs. In addition to identifying component savings it is important to ensure that the duty cycle or operating environment hasn't changed and unknowingly increased the risk of potential product warranty. A positive side effect of cost reduction programs is the reconciliation of old requirements with specifications and identification of any new risks or usages.

Recommended Activities to Support Requirements & Specifications:

- **Confirmation of Customer Requirements**: Working with business development and marketing teams to confirm high-level requirements for the customer facing product. This process also helps identify feature redundancy opportunities for current product but also has the potential to reduce future warranty if customer requirements and duty cycles have unknowingly changed.

- **System Specification Reconciliation:** Working with the engineering teams, it is useful to review the latest requirements and then reconcile with the current engineering specifications to identify any immediate gaps/ opportunities prior to the workshop. It is often beneficial to prioritize this activity around the principle cost drivers

- **Opportunity List:** Construct an opportunity list for features/specifications that may over-exceed requirements and could adversely affect cost.

- **Publish the Requirements:** Cost workshop participants often assume that every feature and associated specification has a necessary function and are regularly unwilling to question its existence. Publishing high level product requirements allows participants to think for themselves and eliminate this common idea generation roadblock. This is a common problem in the automotive industry where features are grandfathered into items such as engine blocks having production lifetimes exceeding in some cases 10 years or more but the features are actually redundant.

Step 3 Outputs:

- *Requirements / Specifications Opportunity list (to support step 4 activities)*

- *Revised requirements document to share with workshop participants containing both system and component level information*

Step 4 - Workshop Facilitation & Savings Generation

The actual cost workshop is the heart of the cost reduction process where the facilitator / cost manager has ultimate responsibility for developing an environment for maximizing the generation of cost savings ideas. Following the workshop, this individual is also tasked with developing a robust plan to deliver these ideas to actual savings realization.

Key Elements in Facilitating a Successful Cost Workshop

Environment & Equipment:

- Identification and selection of a well-lit space free of distractions with adequate space for multiple individuals to comfortably gather but not crowd. Offsite works great for these workshops.

- Providing access to large, clean surfaces to layout components and assemblies for close inspection is important.

- Component drawings and pictures of assemblies should be readily accessible by all participants. Drawings provide detailed insight into materials, specifications, machining processes and tolerances. Hanging prints on the walls for easy reference is always a good idea. Avoid people making assumptions.

- Clipboards and sheets should be provided for participants to capture ideas and should be provided preformatted with sections for:
  - Idea description
  - Estimated savings & confidence factor
  - Implementation probability
  - Estimated tooling investment required
  - Validation requirements
  - Estimated implementation date

- The highlighted product(s) should be available, completely disassembled, thoroughly cleaned, weighed and laid out onto a clean work surface with adequate spacing for people to handle comfortably for close examination.

- Individual component costs developed during Step 1 should be transferred to labels and attached to component for reference. It is important for participants to understand current costs prior to estimating incremental savings. Inexperienced participants can often estimate incremental savings higher than the complete cost of the component.

- Budget permitting, competitive products should be purchased for the purposes of competitive benchmarking. These competitive products should be also fully dismantled and provided as a reference for the workshop participants. It is very insightful for existing product engineers to see how other companies develop specifications to achieve a similar, or better set of requirements.

- For larger assemblies where it is impractical to disassemble and display parts on layout tables, using either a CAD system to walk through an assembly or facilitating the workshop next to the actual hardware is recommended. A CAD walk-through should be utilized as a last resort. Participants tend to be more productive when allowed to handle and examine actual hardware. There is nothing wrong facilitating a cost workshop in a production plant providing appropriate measures have been taken to assure minimal disruption to the surrounding activities.

Personnel Selection - Who Should Participate?

Cross-functional team participation is key for maximum productivity. A significant portion of the savings generated at these workshops often comes from team members not directly involved with the specific product on a day to day basis. A fresh-eyes approach can be very valuable in generating new ideas.

Often, teams working on the specific product being analyzed tend to suffer from tradition-based thinking constraints or the *not-invented-here* conditioning.

Recommended Cost Workshop Invitees Include:

- Product Design
- Manufacturing (Engineering & Technicians)

- Assembly (Engineering & Technicians)
- Product Validation (Test)
- Purchasing
- Sales
- Business Development
- Logistics
- Admin
- External Consultants
- Suppliers
- Actual Product Customers

A product engineering and application expert should be present at each session to answer product or technical questions which participants may have on product requirements and specifications. This individual should provide technical insight but never opinions on the validity of ideas generated by participants.

Maximizing Workshop Participation and Output

- Forcing participation to these events adversely affects productivity. Avoiding the use of "mandatory" in any invitation material is important.

- *"Food-For-Thought"* lunchtime sessions where the company purchases a working, buffet lunch in return for ideas works extremely well. People feel obligated/motivated to generate ideas in return for the company's generosity. There are many examples where $0.50 pizza slices result annual savings of $500K or more (not a bad ROI).

- Exploiting people's curiosity with the excitement of product teardown sessions or competitive benchmarking never fails to draw a crowd. In an effort to foster a sense of excitement, a company-wide e-mail with an invitation weeks before the cost reduction event is highly recommended. In addition, the offer of a free lunch in an invite never fails to draw a large crowd.

- Extending the invitation for participants to attend more than one session is also effective at capturing post workshop ideas. I've observed people participating at sessions for the second and third time generating pages of ideas. For many, the initial session involves learning the process and understanding the expectations, the second and third, capturing the 2am ideas which often carry the highest savings potential.

Maximizing Creativity / Productivity at the Workshop for Participants

- **Promote Working Independently:** An open, vocal, idea sharing forum during workshops is discouraged. The loudest voice tends to dominate. Typically, participants are reluctant to share ideas if there is any risk of public ridicule irrespective of the audience. In addition, these sessions can transform into defensive forums where the engineering team actively defends the current product design.

- **Align Participants with the Requirements:** It is important to present the requirements to the participants and continue to reference these throughout the workshop process. One must ensure to separate specifications from the requirements. Remember, a specification is the technical representation of what the engineering team believes will meet the requirements. Engineering teams are not always correct and often times tend to be conservative in how they develop specifications. Allowing the workshop participants to question the specifications can be very rewarding.

- **100% Idea Capture:** The capturing of all ideas irrespective of how small is the principal objective of the cost workshop. Every idea needs to be captured and processed. Typically, minor ideas are consolidated for validation into a single program and released together for maximum ROI. It is important to explain this to prevent participants running their own ROI calculations and omitting a valid idea.

- **Providing Source of Ideas:** Requesting that participants provide their names should be done for the purpose of follow-up questions only. It can be difficult to interpret handwritten ideas considering the individual was often eating, conceptualizing, writing and walking at the same time.

- **Offering Anonymity:** Fear of ridicule is one of the most powerful ways to dampen productivity during these creative, idea generation events. Participants want praise for the high-value ideas but ridicule is unacceptable for the non-so-good ones. Eliminate this risk.

- **"There is no Bad Idea" Message:** Display this statement on the wall and preach it. The most radical ideas can often provide the greatest savings opportunity. Allow others to be the judge during the post processing efforts.

- **Offering Incentives:** - Rewarding the entire company if the savings meet a predefined target is a great incentive for people to innovate. This has the positive follow-on effect of shifting the culture to having a strong awareness for cost. Rewarding individuals for their specific ideas can result in idea withholding and is generally not a recommended practice.

- **Handwriting:** Sounds like a flippant topic but the most difficult part of the process can often be the facilitator interpreting participants handwriting to accurately record the ideas and associated parameters and metrics following the workshop. Request that the team record their ideas in capitalized text and clearly describe the idea at length.

- **Capturing Late Ideas:** It's important to leave the workshop area intact for a week or so after the workshop officially ends and invite Participants to continue to populate worksheets during that extended period.

- **Provide Cost Reduction Thought Starters:** A standing presentation at the beginning of each workshop session is recommended with shared examples:

  - **Design Optimization:** Is there a more cost-effective design that can achieve the same functional requirements? Does the current design appear to over-achieve the requirements?

  - **Alternative Technologies**: Are there alternative technologies (lower cost) that could meet the same functional requirements?

  - **"Off-The-Shelf" Alternatives**: Is the company manufacturing something which could be replaced by a high volume, low cost, commoditized alternative currently available in the marketplace? Can the system design be modified to accommodate the integration of such a commodity component to reduce complexity and cost?

  - **Component Integration**: Can multiple components be integrated to achieve the same system level function? This is a common opportunity where the engineering team is large or co-located with less than optimal communication resulting in a fragmented, overly complex design.

  - **Alternative Material Selection**: Are there lower cost materials that could be used such as plastics, steels, powdered metals etc.?

  - **Material Specification Alignment**: Is the material specification aligned with the application requirements.

Is there opportunity for cover factor relaxation through the use of alternate material specifications? Does the engineering team understand the current cover factors, so they align with the duty cycle as defined in the requirements? Has the company failed components, developed S/N curves to confirm the validity of cover factors?

- **Machining Optimization**: Deletion of unnecessary machining (eg. casting-in features such as low-tolerance holes instead of machining)

- **Alternative Lower Cost Manufacturing Processes**: Are there lower cost, lower sophistication processes and/or equipment that could be utilized? Is the supply base optimized to meet this fundamental cost requirement?

- **Redundant Feature Deletion**: Do all the features on the component/system provide a specific functional need? If not, can they be eliminated?

- **Raw Material Drop Shipping / Contract Pricing**: Can raw materials be purchased and dropped-shipped to the machining supplier leveraging economies of scale and avoiding additional handling fees and mark-up?

- **Tolerance Relaxation**: Are there any tolerances on the print that could be relaxed? Tolerances can be significant, hidden cost drivers. Does the team understand the cost sensitivity of specific tolerances and the real cost savings opportunity if they are relaxed? Would a simple tolerance stack-up validate the opportunity? If sub-components within a sub-assembly require excessively tight tolerances can the sub-assembly itself be final machined externally post assembly to relax this need?

- **Critical and Significant Characteristics**: Are these appropriately identified and called-out on prints as these drive inspection requirements and therefore cost? Can CCc and SCs be eliminated? It is quite common for SCs and CCs to be haphazardly generated and included on prints. One must stick to the appropriate FMEA generation methodology to avoid unnecessary costs.

- **Commonization & Complexity Reduction**: Can components be commonized to reduce complexity? Fasteners are a common opportunity for complexity reduction initiatives. Cascading a list of acceptable fasteners at the beginning of a product development process can be extremely beneficial. Even with a commonly dimensioned fastener, surface finishes and strength grades can generate significant, unnecessary complexity and cost.

- **Beautification Features**: Do components / assemblies really need to look attractive? Can coatings be eliminated, or specifications relaxed? Will the customer ever see the component or care how it really looks?

- **Sealing**: Are there alternative lower cost gaskets available. Can gaskets be replaced with RTV sealant?

- **Overseas Sourcing**: Are there cost savings opportunities in procuring components from overseas sources?

- **Warranty Reduction**: Is it possible to redesign the component to reduce warranty? Holistic thinking is important.

- **Warranty Cost Sharing**: Is the component cost artificially high due to current warranty agreements and associated accrual? Is it possible to re-write warranty policies to lower component costs? This is often a prudent analysis to conduct when the product is established in the market and warranty has stabilized.

- **End of Line Testing**: Is the EOL test driving significant cost, can the requirements be relaxed based on product maturity and manufacturing experience? For years, every automotive engine was tested as it rolled off the production line, this is no longer the case. There are lower cost ways to infer a problem during the assembly process instead of expensive EOL testing.

Step 5 – Capturing & Organizing the Data

The list described below represents the output categories from the workshop as captured on the worksheets and must be recorded in a spreadsheet for further processing and analysis by the facilitator / cost manager (described in chapter 4)

Captured Data From Workshop:

- Idea description
- Estimated savings & confidence factor
- Implementation probability (risk assessment)
- Estimated tooling investment required
- Validation requirements
- Estimated implementation timing

Chapter 4 - Workshop Data Processing

This is traditionally the point at which many of these processes fail.

Although the workshop may have been a tremendous success with hundreds of ideas generated, it is critical to maintain the momentum by processing the data generated and initiating the actual cost reduction projects. Remember the company doesn't realize cost savings until an idea is released into production. This is a common pitfall at this stage of the process.

It's important to realize that the raw data generated during the cost workshop is highly subjective and must be carefully processed. An appropriate level of technical and commercial due diligence must be applied by both the engineering and sourcing teams to ensure that opportunities are valid, and savings estimates correctly weighted. The initial step in this process is the organization of data into a format that allows for easy manipulation and sorting. The objective final output being a list of prioritized, actionable projects with a timeline demonstrating a credible cost reduction and cost savings roadmap.

Step 1: Developing the Core Idea Spreadsheet

The cost reduction spreadsheet is the single point of reference for the entire cost reduction initiative, it is important to avoid excessive sophistication to ensure that the contents are clear and easy to read but most importantly easy to modify and track by multiple end users. Keep it simple.

Column Headings / Data Management: Within the spreadsheet, specific column headings should be generated to assist in the prioritization and the general management of the data. Others are a matter of preference and can be unique depending on the company and product type.

Recommended Spreadsheet Column Headings

Identifier	Formula
A	Idea No.
B	Idea Description
C	Idea Type (eg. Design / Supply Chain)
D	Idea Owner
E	Implementation Probability (0-1)
F	Estimated Savings Per Component
G	Savings Confidence (0-1)
H	Weighted Savings Per Component
I	No. Units Per Assembly
J	Total Savings Per Assembly
K	Annual Volumes
L	Annual Savings
M	Validation Test Description
N	Validation Time Requirements
O	Validation Cost (Test Stands, Prototypes)
P	Production Tooling Investment
Q	Total Implementation Cost
R	Estimated Implementation Timing
S	Timing for Savings Realization

Spreadsheet Calculations: Traditionally with this type of project there is little need for sophisticated calculations apart from the application of weighting factors such as Implementation Probability and Savings Confidence (E & G).

Key Calculations

Principal Calculations	Formula
H (Savings Per Component)	= E * F * G
J (Total Savings per Assembly)	= H * I
L (Annual Savings)	= J * K
Q (Total Implementation Cost)	= O + P
S (Timing for Savings Realization)	= Q / L

Step 2: Initial Savings Validation

Where feasible, all ideas and savings estimates should be scrutinized and sanitized by the cost manager prior to presenting to the broader team and steering committee for the purpose of consensus and prioritization. Pricing research of similar feature examples in production and supplier interaction can be leveraged to develop estimates, probabilities and confidence ratings. High level calculations such as $/lb or $/Kg can be a useful, rapid method to develop notional savings estimates especially for ideas involving alternate materials or material removal.

Savings validation is an iterative process as suppliers increase their level of participation and provide greater data granularity.

Step 3: Generating Group Consensus

With the draft of the spreadsheet complete, the core group should review and collectively update the critical parameters in the spreadsheet to determine savings potential and relative implementation priorities for each idea. Items such as savings estimates, implementation probabilities and validation strategies (such as idea consolidation) are key.

It is typical in these types of exercises to expect significant updates during the group review so it's important to allocate sufficient time to ensure that all vested parties are aligned, and post meeting implementation can begin without fundamental disagreements or resistance that traditionally delay progress in these types of projects. Risk tends to be the principal product trade-off attribute during these events.

Step 4: Timing Plan Creation

The timing plan is the schedule management tool that the cost reduction program manager will develop and use throughout the process to drive idea implementation to a specific timeline in an effort to achieve the desired savings curve. As a change agent, it is important to document key decision milestones and have a plan granular enough to track individual organizational actives on a weekly basis. Elevating cost reduction projects to the same tracking scrutiny as traditional product development activities should be encouraged by the steering committee.

Chapter 5 - Implementation & Savings Realization

For the majority of organizations irrespective of size or product type, implementation becomes the most challenging phase of the cost reduction process. Many companies have databases of cost opportunities but little actual realized savings. There seems to be a subconscious sense of accomplishment following the generation of ideas, but the process can typically halt during the critical transition phase to product development and sourcing. This is one of the principal reasons why a Cost Manager must facilitate the process from idea development through to implementation.

Without the transformation of ideas into realized savings, the process has limited or no value. There are a variety of reasons why the process can fail but there are numerous ways and methods to guarantee its success.

Guaranteeing Idea Implementation Success

Recommendation 1: Process Ownership

A recurring theme in this publication but a single individual within the organization must be responsible for the cost reduction program from concept through to implementation. A common pitfall occurs when traditional cost workshop facilitators transfer ownership to engineering and/or sourcing following the idea spreadsheet development. Lack of ownership at this stage almost guarantees that the process will stall. Having a neutral, non-engineering or sourcing individual with performance metrics linked to actual savings realization and not just idea generation is essential to ensure maximum realization of identified savings.

Recommendation 2: Key Personnel Selection

Although the position of cost manager can be perceived as a peripheral, non-critical position, one must never underestimate how important it is to ensure that the individual chosen has the personality, experience and perseverance that align with the demanding needs of that job. This role is for the experienced and self-motivated individuals only.

Attributes of a Great Cost Manager:

People Skills: Individuals must be able to establish and maintain strong relationships between all organizations especially engineering and supply chain. Without the appropriate amount of support from these organizations the cost reduction program manager cannot be successful, and the process can fail. Keeping an independent, objective position (non-biased) in this type of relationship management role is key.

Technical Skills: Strong technical competence is a tremendous asset to overcome the continuous stream of roadblocks that can typically be encountered during project feasibility assessment, kick-off, validation and actual implementation. Having a technically objective and experienced cost manager in this type of role can help in the removal of challenging roadblocks. The ability to develop creative ways to design and validate ideas is key enabling the success of even the most challenging and radical of ideas.

Commercial Knowledge: Having insight into cost estimation, sourcing strategies, commercial agreements, product and implementation costs is an obvious skill that pays dividends in this type of role. Developing sophisticated cost models and developing creative ways to manage finances can often make the difference between an idea's success or failure.

Recommendation 3: Rigid Project Management

Each project must have a detailed task list and an associated gant chart. The cost manager is responsible for creating timelines collaboratively with engineering and supply chain and then driving the implementation of these projects in a traditional manner. Being able to create and run projects to realistic timelines, providing weekly status updates to steering committees is critical to driving projects to completion on time.

Recommendation 4: Regular Reporting / Roadblock Removal

Relative to traditional projects, cost reduction initiatives require significant policing and regular roadblock removal. To accelerate the success of cost reduction programs (realized savings), a weekly report-out to a steering committee can be instrumental. Having leadership support with budget authority is recommended. A weekly report presented by the cost manager to the steering committee incorporating status updates and project roadblocks forces rapid resolution and drives the process forward towards completion.

Chapter 6 - Idea Validation & Risk Mitigation

Mechanical validation testing can become the single largest roadblock in most cost reduction programs principally due to the associated costs and timing. Because of the financial risk that mechanical validation poses to savings realization, it is important to thoroughly investigate alternate more cost effective validation options. Spending the appropriate amount of time developing an optimized validation strategy that reduces cost and time resulting in the enabling of valuable ideas by providing an acceptable ROI is time well spent.

Mechanical validation testing, validation through analysis or simply signing off a new design by similitude to an old design are all options available to the engineering team and all must be considered as enablers to getting ideas into production as quickly as possible at the lowest cost and of course with minimal risk. Ultimately, validation testing decisions are the responsibility of the engineering team.

Typical Validation Methodologies

Validation Using Analysis

With today's advanced Finite Element Analysis (FEA) and Computational Fluid Dynamics (CFD) tools it is possible to accurately simulate the functional and durability characteristics of most components providing the boundary conditions are well understood. In cases where they are not, instrumentation of the application can quickly generate the appropriate levels of information needed.

For incremental design changes, the analysis process is relatively quick. If the original analysis was correlated to the application or the mechanical testing, the conclusions from the incremental design changes can provide high levels of confidence. In many cases where cover factors remain unchanged, there may be little need for further mechanical verification testing.

Mechanical Validation

Traditional testing with large statistical sample sizes, high resource and timing demands do not lend themselves to the cost and timing needs of typical cost reduction programs.

However, there are numerous ways to conduct mechanical validation testing that minimize both cost and timing and still deliver high levels of confidence.

Tails Testing: This methodology is an enabler to quickly building high levels of confidence using a relatively small sample size.

This approach requires the engineering team to procure components at worse case tolerance conditions and test these components with worst case noise factors.

Worse case tolerance condition examples:

- Minimal material (lowest strength)
- Worst case material specification (lowest strength)
- Worst case surface finish (fatigue factors)

Worse case noise factor examples:

- Maximum bending, tension & shock loads
- Maximum and minimum temperatures
- Thermal Shock
- High corrosion
- Operating at resonant frequency (assuming it occurs within duty cycle)
- High Frequency

Care must always be taken to ensure that tolerances and noise factors are appropriately selected to ensure that the results are in fact worst-case.

Application Testing: For components in non-critical applications and in situations where a good relationship exists with a customer there is little to replace real life application testing.

Offering incentives to customers who understand and agree to any testing risks can be a great way to test enabling the hardware to experience real life noise factors at minimal cost. Detailed damage analysis from components on test can be used to correlate any analysis performed.

The downside of this approach is that it takes time and field engineering resources to monitor the progress of these components.

Other Methodologies to Accelerate Validation Testing

- Destructive Testing - S/N Curve Comparison
- HALT (Highly Accelerated Life Test) / HASS (Highly Accelerated Stress Screening)
- Damage Model Development (development of an algorithm that represents component damage as a function of duty cycle)

Chapter 7 - Organizational Cost Awareness

For many organizations, cost reduction projects are often initiated post product launch when the unacceptable gap between cost and price is ultimately realized and engineering resources become available to support the "re-engineering for cost" activities. Unfortunately, there many issues and challenges associated with this type of traditional approach.

Post Launch Cost Reduction Challenges

- Product tooling monies have been invested (many companies invest millions of dollars in hard tooling, often with a 5-7 year amortization period). Many post Job-1 cost reduction ideas are deemed not feasible because of the re-investment required for new tooling.

- Product validation has been completed at considerable expense. Re-validation would not support a positive ROI.

- Engineering teams are suffering post launch burn-out from supporting product launch activities.

- Accelerated testing often conducted to reduce validation costs for post Job-1 changes could increase the risk of problems and product warranty. Deviating radically from the original design compounds this risk.

Creating the Culture for Concurrent Cost Optimization

From facilitating multiple cost reduction initiatives over the course of many decades, the primary reason for even needing a cost reduction initiative was due to the lack of cost sensitivity awareness during the product development process.

Recommendations for Future Product Development Programs

- Mandatory integration of target cost as a functional requirement in key program documentation from program kick-off. This documentation includes formal requirements documents and FMEAs (Concept and Design).

- Development of cost models for all components irrespective of how insignificant. It's common for the minor items to get missed and have an adverse impact at the end of a program.

- Integration of cost models and curves in engineering specification documentation proving that the design aligns with the cost targets.

- Application of "should-cost" analysis toolsets throughout the product development process to validate cost models and cost curves. More importantly, "should-cost" analysis can direct the design efforts to the lowest cost solutions.

- Active cost benchmarking of competitive products throughout the design process.

- Application of advanced CAE tools and methodologies for topology optimization and material content reduction.

- Regular cost workshops with internal and external participants.

- Facilitation of cost workshops at supplier facilities with exposure and understanding of key manufacturing cost drivers.

- Engagement of technical and cost reduction consultants for specific expertise.

- Creating a culture of emotional separation from the design and the willingness to iterate and adopt alternate technologies if the current selection doesn't align with the cost targets.

Integration of cost optimization into the DNA of most companies can be accomplished over time by increasing cost awareness through education and the application of readily available, proven tools and methodologies.

Section B - Chronic Problem Resolution

Chapter 8 - Introduction – Problem Resolution

Problems erode margins. Perhaps its laziness or just a function of human nature but for most of us it's quite common for the instant gratification experienced from symptom relief to dampen our motivation for understanding the true root cause of most problems. Only when the recurrence becomes frequent or the effects of a problem excessively discomforting do we typically give root cause even the slightest consideration. We conveniently confuse short term interim solutions with true root cause resolution because masking symptoms is typically much easier and perceived to be sufficiently adequate rather than solving problems.

Interim solutions or the masking of symptoms has an important role in the problem resolution process. The principal purpose of this step should be to provide immediate protection to the parties experiencing the symptoms or effects of a problem while providing adequate time to properly identify and verify the true root cause. The objective of any problem resolution activity should be to ensure that the optimum, lowest cost, most robust long-term solution is both identified and implemented. This applies irrespective of problem type. Misinterpretation of interim solutions as permanent solutions is the most common pitfall individuals or organizations experience when trying to solve complex problems. Proof of process failure is problem recurrence with all the associated negative side effects.

Interim solutions are temporary because by their very nature they carry side effects. It can be the side effect of increased product cost driven by the addition of a new product feature. It can be a medical side effect of a drug used to treat the symptoms of an underlying problem. It's important to minimize reliance on interim solutions for anything longer than is necessary to identify the true root cause. Ignoring this approach can result in interim solutions being used to mask the symptoms of previous interim solutions resulting in a runaway, self-perpetuating process. When a product falls foul to this runaway process, costs increase, functionality decreases, and products slowly lose market competitiveness. This is graphically described in the illustration below.

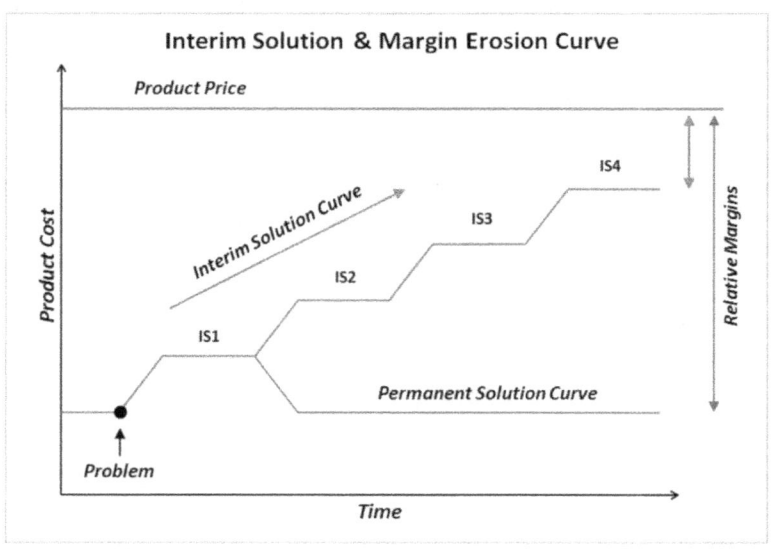

Having individuals in an organization who are proficient at problem resolution is a tremendous asset and can have a demonstrable impact on a company's margin, speed to market, product robustness and subsequent growth. In addition to resolving issues with current products, the philosophy and methodology described in this book also applies to any challenging problem experienced during the product development cycle. Early detection and rapid resolution influence the reduction in costs and ensures successful product launches.

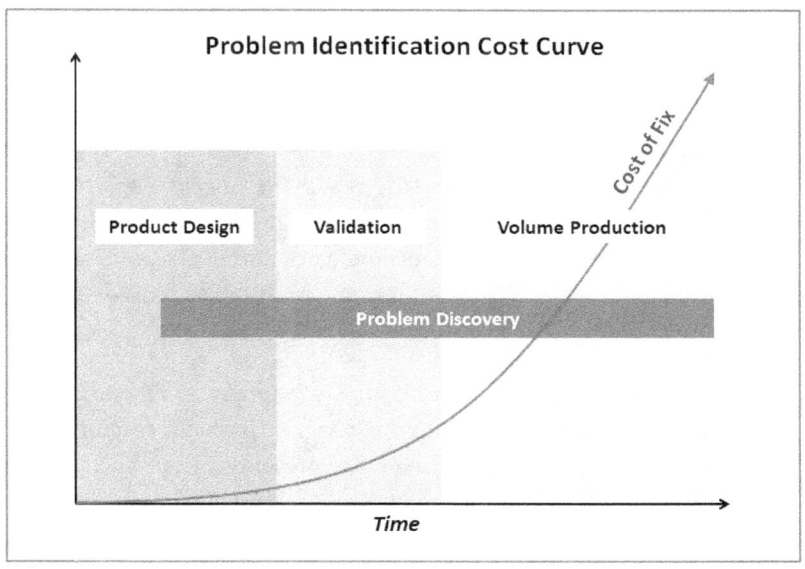

Chapter 9 - Problem Resolution Lessons Learned

The phrase "Lessons Learned" has instilled itself in the DNA of most organizations over the past twenty years. The principle objective behind the process is to prevent organizations from repeating past mistakes and enable the continuous improvement of products and/or services. Unfortunately, the process itself is rarely executed to realize its maximum potential.

The intention of this chapter is to share problem resolution process lessons learned accumulated during years of problem resolution project facilitation. These lessons learned are presented prior to the in-depth process review to allow the reader to consider their integration as the process is further described.

Problem Resolution Process Lessons Learned

Facilitation: Relying on just a process alone to solve a complex problem without experienced project leadership almost always results in process failure. The methodology of facilitation can be just as important as the core problem resolution process itself. Identification and selection of an experienced process facilitator is essential to the success of the overall process and the pace at which results are achieved. This is why many organizations despite having comprehensive training in quality systems and associated methods still elect to hire external resources to facilitate high profile problem resolution projects.

Subject Matter Expertise is not Essential: A common misconception most organizations have is that the facilitator of a problem resolution project must be a subject matter expert for the product or subject being addressed. It actually helps objectivity if the individual is not. Appointing a technical lead to the role of facilitator can introduce a counterproductive bias in the process from the very beginning. Ignorance of the subject matter can actually assist the facilitator in remaining unbiased and data driven.

The Core Team: Like any project, the quality of the output has a direct correlation to the quality of the team working on it. Although convenient to deploy the B or C teams, these types of demanding projects are mostly suited for A team type individuals. Having a high caliber team working on these projects will pay dividends when one considers the savings associated with rapid resolution.

Expect Resistance: A facilitator must always be prepared for resistance from team members. Every project possesses one individual who passionately believes they know what the root cause is from the very beginning of the process. One must always remember that proof of root cause identification is the ability to turn on an off the problem under controlled conditions. Until this has been demonstrated repeatedly, at will, the problem and associated root cause remains alive and well.

Objectivity not Subjectivity: As a facilitator and participant, rigid objectivity in how we analyze problems and gauge success is one of the most important attributes needed to drive the process to a successful outcome. Forcing individuals to embrace a data driven mindset is necessary to eliminate all subjective influences that have a strong tendency to derail these types of processes. Every phase of the problem resolution process is vulnerable to derailment. Using objectivity and a reliance on data to drive decisions is essential to ensure the process stays on course.

Parallel Activities for Maximum Effectiveness: If timing is a critical element and resources are available then the process steps of interim and permanent solution development should always be conducted in parallel. In addition to accelerating the project completion, this technique also prevents the common issue of interim and permanent solution cross contamination. One must remember that interim and permanent solutions are never intended to be the same. Differentiating these is important for maximum process effectiveness and expeditious results.

Chapter 10 - Process Overview

The process described in this book is a derivative of one successfully used for many years in various industries and is responsible for millions of dollars in product savings through rapid, complex problem resolution. The application possibilities for this methodology are endless both inside and even outside of work. As is described in the graphic below, where feasible, steps 2 and 3 should always be run in parallel.

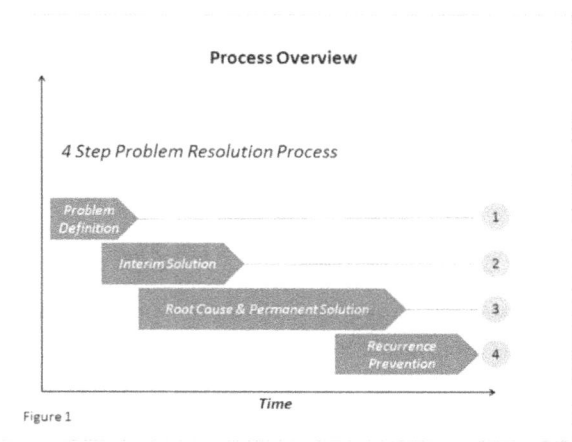

Figure 1

The Problem Resolution Process

Basic Process Steps:

Step 1: *Problem Definition*

Step 2: *Interim Solution Development - Symptom Relief*

Step 3: *Root Cause Identification and Permanent Solution Development*

Step 4: *Recurrence Prevention*

Step 1: Problem Definition sets the framework for the project and subsequent activities. This deceptively simple appearing step is actually quite complex and sets the framework for the entire project. Get it wrong and the process is almost guaranteed to fail.

Step 2: Interim Solution focuses on developing rapid solutions to mask the symptoms of a problem irrespective of the root cause. Interim solutions should never be misinterpreted as permanent solutions. It is very rare for an interim solution to satisfy the criteria of a permanent solution. The interim solution is not expected to identify or resolve the root cause.

Step 3: Root Cause and Permanent Solution establishes a framework to identify and verify the root cause. Success is measured on the ability to repeatedly turn on and off the problem under controlled conditions. There is no flexibility in this acceptance criteria.

Step 4: Recurrence Prevention forces the project team to examine the organizational and/or process gaps that allowed the problem to occur. It then forces the participants to develop safeguards to prevent similar types of problems from recurring in the future.

Problem Resolution Team Essentials

A - Facilitator: *Manages and Coaches the Project Team*

- Highly motivated individual, objective and data driven

- Strong at driving innovation and managing personalities

- Individual can be internal or external

- Must be available to devote 100% of time to run the project

B - Core Team: *Continuously Supporting the Project*

- Product experts who understand the current product design, requirements and specifications

- Customer facing individuals closest to the problem with access to raw data generated by customers

- Validation experts to assist in problem recreation and solution validation

C- Peripheral Team: *Intermittently Supporting the Project as Needed*

- **Sales and Marketing** to support the roll-out of interim and permanent solutions

- **Purchasing** to support cost model development and expedited prototype procurement

- **Manufacturing** to support the development of high volume, robust solutions (DFM)

- **Controls and Software** to support the creation of software solutions. Regularly, hardware shortfalls can be robustly masked by software solutions. One should always keep controls and software experts close at hand.

Problem Resolution Project Timing

The length of any problem resolution project is unique and depends on a variety of factors typically unique for each project. However, some guidelines are provided below to help address this common question.

Step 1 – Problem Resolution ~ 2 Days: Describing the problem is not as remedial a task as one might think. Making a mistake at this stage can derail the entire process and result in significant resource wastage and project delay. Spending at least two days on this step is not unusual.

Step 2 – Interim Solution Development ~ 6 Weeks: This timing includes brainstorming, rapid prototype development, procurement, testing and roll-out. Remember, this assumes the A-team and adequate, responsive resource availability to support immediate needs.

Step 3 – Root Cause and Permanent Solution ~ 12 Weeks: It is assumed that this process will run in parallel with the interim solution development. The objective is to have a permanent solution offering available 6 weeks after the interim solution is in place.

Step 4 – Recurrence Prevention: Because this falls under the umbrella of continuous improvement it is usually an on-going process. Integrating the learning's from a specific problem should not take more than a week.

Chapter 11 - Defining the Problem

Often misinterpreted as a trivial task, the procedure of defining the problem can be the most important step in the problem resolution process. Failure to spend adequate time on this step can result in process derailment. Unfortunately, this quite common process pitfall often results in teams spending time and resources resolving the wrong problem.

The task of generating the problem statement itself must be allocated sufficienct time to prepare and validate. A good problem statement clearly captures detailed situational information, the symptoms of the problem and any known, quantified effects. It captures the "real" problem. A poor problem statement captures vague descriptions, assumes both symptoms and their effects and confuses hypotheses with fact.

Good & Bad Problem Statement Examples

(These examples are fictitious for the purposes of process coaching only)

Scenario 1:

A vehicle OEM is experiencing high warranty costs and increasing customer dissatisfaction. Initial reports from the field indicate that customers are observing smoke coming from the engine compartment of their vehicles. Customers are taking their vehicles to dealerships for repeated, unsuccessful repair which is driving high warranty costs and customer dissatisfaction. There is a risk of bad PR for the organization if this issue is not quickly resolved.

Bad Problem Statement 1:

"Customer Engines are smoking, faulty engine breather"

What's bad about this Problem Statement?

- Description is vague
- There is an assumed, unsubstantiated root cause included in the problem statement. Focusing prematurely on this as a root cause will risk derailing the entire process. This is a surprisingly common occurrence as individuals are added to a project assuming that the root cause has been validated.
- This problem statement focuses on the technical issue only. The effects of the problem are missing.
- There is no information relative to the magnitude of the problem or the actual symptoms experienced by both the customers or the company dealing with the effects of the problem.

Good Problem Statement 1:

"Visible customer smoke from front of vehicles after vehicle warms up on low mileage 2012MY and later vehicle type X resulting in customer dealership visits and warranty claims in the region of ~$100,000 per day. Reports of customer dissatisfaction due to problem recurrence following initial repair is reaching automotive blog and media sites posing a brand image risk"

What's Good:

- Addresses real problem (daily costs, customer dissatisfaction, bad company PR)

- Provides symptom information as the customer observes it. Provides insight into how customer experiences the symptoms of the problem.
- Provides good insight into the magnitude of the problem and the actual potential effects of the problem for the company

The Benefit of a Good Problem Statement

A good problem statement provides clear insight to the team about the problem and sets the stage for developing robust interim and long-term permanent solutions.

Scenario 2:

A prototype technology demonstration machine has failed 3 days before an investor review committee meeting, jeopardizing release of tranche funding. The machine has 8 electrical panels, 2 of which have failed. The machine will be unable to operate at peak performance to demonstrate the maximum process efficiency. There is no feasible way to replace the specialty panels in the available timeframe due to lengthy manufacturing lead times.

Bad Problem Statement 1:

"Electrical panels have failed, the machine is non-operational"

What's bad about this Problem Statement?

- Focuses solely on the technical aspects of the problem
- Doesn't address the true symptoms of the problem or real side effects and potential consequences for the company
- Doesn't provide insight into how long the machine will be down
- Implies the issue originated at the electrical panels. Failed electrical panels may just be a symptom of an underlying root cause.

Good Problem Statement 1:

"Unable to demonstrate the machines maximum performance and efficiency to investors in the required timeframe due to a major hardware failure. Hardware will take three months to repair. Root cause is unknown but electrical panels are indicating malfunctions. Consequence of this failure is the risk to the securing of tranche funding for the company to keep operating at current capacity"

What's Good:

- Identifies the immediate symptom of the problem - risk to the tranche funding and basic survival of the company. This immediately is elevated to the executive level and enables them to react and develop potentially non-hardware related interim solutions.
- Provides information regarding time to procure replacement parts but also includes a statement that the root cause is unknown.

The importance of correctly defining the problem statement cannot be over emphasized and should be revisited daily by the project facilitator to ensure it remains current. It requires continuous validation as additional data is gathered and processed from the field.

Chapter 12 - Interim Solution Development

An interim solution is a temporary but highly effective method of protecting the customer from the symptoms of a problem and equally importantly, protecting the party responsible for the product or service from the immediate effects of that problem. An interim solution is intended as mechanism to secure the team working on the root cause sufficient time to develop a robust, optimized and fully validated solution to address the root cause. An interim solution should never be mistaken for a permanent solution because interim solutions typically carry adverse side effects. The interim solution process is designed to identify, develop and rank each interim solution option in terms of potential effectiveness and associated side effects. These prioritized solutions are validated and rolled out to the field as quickly as possible.

Consider this simple example: An individual's car has broken down. A typical, reactive way of defining this as a problem statement is the *"car has broken down"*. Many teams would immediately start focusing on the car to figure out ways to fix it while the frustrated customer waits patiently for a solution. However, an interim solution focused team would immediately address the symptoms of the problem which is *lack of mobility* for the customer and determine ways to rapidly address these symptoms before focusing on the root cause.

In this example, possible interim solution options include:

- *Taxi*
- *Rental Car*
- *Garage Loaner*

Each of the interim solution options listed above carry different side effects but alleviate the symptoms of the problem for the customer.

Side Effects:

- *Taxi* - Expensive, inconvenient
- *Rental Car* - Expensive, may require collection and drop-off
- *Garage Loaner* - Convenient, low cost for customer, no time limit *(note that this interim solution carries potential costs for the OEM but a loaner car may be less expensive than repeated warranty repairs)*

Clearly, the ideal interim solution for the customer is the garage loaner. It immediately addresses the lack of mobility issue for the customer and carries minimal side effects. It does nothing to address the root cause of the problem which is perfectly acceptable at this stage.

Common Interim Solution Process Pitfalls

- **Confusing Interim & Permanent Solutions:** The most common pitfall in the problem resolution process occurs when teams confuse interim solutions with permanent solutions. Even experienced team members can fall foul to focusing on root cause while trying to develop interim solutions. This frequently results in an artificially long interim solution development process, significantly reducing its effectiveness potential.

- **Combining Interim and Permanent Solutions:** Teams intentionally combine interim and permanent solutions in an effort to try to simplify and accelerate the process. Unfortunately, this doesn't work:

- Symptoms last longer than desired resulting in high costs for the product producer and extended symptom periods for the customer. Permanent solutions typically take longer to develop than interim solutions.
- Risk of problem recurrence and compounded costs if the release of a permanent solution has been accelerated and inadequately validated.

- **Mask the Symptoms:** Teams forget that interim solutions need only mask the symptoms of a problem. Interim solutions can typically be developed without any understanding of the root cause. There should be little need to discuss root cause hypotheses.

- **Interim Solution Becomes the Permanent Solution.** Side effects from interim solutions can result in other issues if relied upon as a long-term solution. In addition, since the root cause is not resolved, other symptoms from the root cause may also arise.

- **Interim Solution is Released with Insufficient Validation.** The premature release of inadequately validated interim solutions can cause new problems in addition to the original set being addressed.

A Good Interim Solution:

- Easy and quick to develop
- Low cost
- Easy to validate
- Low risk of adverse side effects
- Easy to implement
- Minimal investment
- Must not degrade overall product performance
- Presence must be imperceptible by the customer

- Easy to remove at a later date and replace with an optimized permanent solution when available

A Poor Interim Solution:

- Complex and difficult to develop
- Expensive
- Requires extensive, lengthy validation, delaying time to market
- Requires significant investment
- Difficult to implement
- Numerous adverse side effects perceptible by customers
- Difficult to remove at a later date

One of the most effective methods of generating interim solution options is a group idea brainstorming workshop. The output of this workshop is a list of ranked, prioritized ideas requiring further investigation and validation.

Interim Solution Workshop Process

Step 1 – Core Team Selection

Selecting the appropriate team is the first critical step in the brainstorming process. Unlike the permanent solution process, the interim solution process relies on creativity and innovation. This is not intended to be an engineering intense exercise; it is merely an investigation in effectively masking the symptoms irrespective of how sophisticated and elusive the problem appears to be. Because this is an exercise in creativity, tapping into a broad array of experience and disciplines is essential to generating as many ideas as possible. One must always remember that the team objective is not to determine root cause; it is merely to mask the symptoms the customer is experiencing. Radical and creative ideas are always welcome.

Customer interface/support individuals are important to this part of the process to ensure that the symptoms as described are correct and that the proposed interim solution options are ranked capturing customer acceptance potential.

Interim Solution Workshop Participants

Workshop Participation Can Include:

- Design
- Manufacturing (Engineering & Technicians)
- Assembly (Engineering & Technicians
- Purchasing
- Sales & Marketing
- Business Development
- Logistics
- Admin
- External Consultants
- Suppliers
- Product Customers
- Product Users (Customers)

Step 2 – Symptom Definition

Every customer will have a slightly different interpretation of the symptoms of any problem. Having comprehensive insight into these symptoms is critical during the workshop. These symptoms should be tabulated and used to support the interim solution prioritization process.

Step 3 – Brainstorming Workshop

Similar to any brainstorming workshop, establishing the ground rules is important to maximize creativity and productivity of the participants. In addition, leveraging a broad audience with a diversity of backgrounds and perspectives will always maximize the volume and quality of ideas generated.

Key workshop ground rules:

- All participants have a thorough understanding of the symptoms. It is the job of the facilitator to ensure that the participants are appropriately informed of the key details.

- There are no bad ideas, all ideas generated will be captured and processed irrespective of how radical they may appear.

- Ranking occurs after the brainstorming session. It is important to avoid judging ideas until all ideas are captured.

Step 4 – Population of Interim Solution Template & Ranking Process

During the idea generation workshop, the facilitator usually develops an interim solution ranking matrix (as shown below). It is important to use a spreadsheet with data sorting features as the process of ranking is an iterative process. One should expect the ranking to change as the validation process progresses. Following the workshop, subjective ideas will transition to objective ones as data becomes available.

Interim Solution Workshop Prioritization Template

A	B	C	D	E	F	G
Idea No.	Idea Description	Estimated Effectiveness (0-10)	Implementation Time (0-10)	Ease of Implementation (0-10)	Cost (0-10)	Total
1	Description	0-10 10 = Good	0-10 10 = Short Time	0-10 10 = Easy	0-10 10 = Low Cost	Value = Product (C-F)

Categories explained:

- **A – Idea No.:** Method of managing and identifying the ideas.

- **B - Idea Description:** Clear description of the idea with sufficient detail to enable the document to be circulated to non-participants for further analysis and input.
- **C - Estimated Effectiveness:** A subjective team ranking of the potential effectiveness of the interim solution being analyzed. 0 being a low potential effectiveness, 10 being high.
- **D - Implementation Time:** A relative assessment of implementation time for the idea being proposed. 0 representing a long time relative to 10 which represents a rapid implementation.
- **E - Ease of Implementation:** The ease at which an idea can be implemented in the field. This takes into consideration design time, validation time even hands-on product retrofitting in the field. 0 represents a lengthy process of implementation, 10 equates to rapid implementation.
- **F- Cost of Implementation:** Relative ranking of estimated cost associated with each interim solution implementation effort. These costs include product development costs in addition to roll-out. 0 represents a high cost, 10 a low cost solution.
- **G- Total:** This is the ultimate ranking metric. It is simply the product of C to F for each idea. Weighting the rankings is also an option not illustrated here.

These relative rankings will change in the first few days of a project as new discoveries are made and subjective estimates transition to objective data.

Step 5 – Solution Validation

Typically, the top 3 interim solutions as developed during the ranking process are selected for parallel validation. Because of the nature of the interim solution, this process should take days and not weeks.

Validation can be a combination of physical testing and analytical testing. The ultimate test is the validation on a unit exhibiting the problem in the field.

Step 6 – Solution Roll Out

As soon as the ideas has been appropriately internally validated to prove symptom relief with a statistically acceptable sample size, it is important to verify that the introduction of this interim solution does not create other potential issues in the field. As soon as feasible, representative team members should be in the field performing product retrofits and validating on units that have demonstrated the failure mode being addressed.

Following retrofitting activities and effectiveness validation, the task becomes a carefully coordinated field roll-out depending on the specific characteristics of the original problem.

Step 7 – Solution Monitoring

Because interim solutions can carry side effects, it is important to ensure the nature and magnitude of these side effects are fully understood. Careful monitoring of units in the field should always be conducted until a permanent solution is ready for release.

Chapter 13 - Root Cause Identification & Permanent Solution Development

The principle objective behind any problem resolution initiative is the rapid identification of the root cause of a problem with the subsequent development of an optimized and fully validated solution. Because of the intensive resource loading these projects typically place on organizations, problem resolution activities are often terminated prematurely before hypotheses have been adequately validated. The consequence of early process termination can be problem recurrence.

Rule of Root Cause Identification:

"Proof that a root cause has been identified and validated is the ability to repeatedly turn on and off the problem at will under controlled conditions"

Common Root Cause Process Lessons Learned

- **Without Data, it's just a Hypothesis:** Irrespective of the knowledge or passion an individual might have for the subject matter, every idea must be categorized as an unproven hypothesis until data exists to prove otherwise. Dealing with strong personalities who want to shortcut the process is a common challenge during these types of projects. Remaining rigidly objective and insisting on supporting data is essential to manage these types of common process disruptions.

- **Quality & Knowledge of the Team:** Building the correct team with the appropriate skillset and experience is vital for the process to have maximum effectiveness. Companies are often unwilling to dedicate the "A" team due to conflicting commitments with other pressing needs. However, it is a commitment that always pays dividends. The problem resolution process doesn't function well with prolonged knowledge or data gaps. Taking the time necessary to establish and maximize a team's core competency relative to the subject matter is vital. In addition to technical expertise, having individuals with direct field knowledge of the problem and associated symptoms is also important for establishing the facts directly from the customers perspective.

- **Don't Short Cut Root Cause Prove Out:** Time to failure can often be unknowingly extended by changes made during the hypotheses prove-out process. It's quite common for this change to failure time to be misinterpreted as actual resolution of the root cause. Teams must always remain disciplined and rely on the litmus test of repeatedly turning on and off the problem under controlled conditions to validate that the root cause has in fact been resolved. This is a very common pitfall for projects with budget constraints.

- **Experienced Facilitator Selection:** Even the most seasoned of facilitators can struggle to manage problem resolution projects objectively and effectively. This is why companies regularly tend to engage outside consultant experts to facilitate these processes despite having comprehensive training in the tools and processes of problem resolution.

- **Steering Committee:** A facilitator alone, especially an external consultant isn't typically empowered to make product design, investment or resourcing decisions. The facilitator needs to be held accountable to timing and quality of the project output. Having a Steering Committee established to monitor progress, remove roadblocks and authorize spend is critical to maximize the speed and success of projects. Typical interaction with steering committees should be at least weekly. The steering committee typically comprises of two to three individuals empowered to make decisions and remove progress roadblocks.

Root Cause Toolset and Process Steps

Step 1 – Core Team Selection

The team working on root cause can differ significantly from that working on interim solution. In the case of root cause there is less reliance on creativity and significantly more focus on subject matter expertise.

Root Cause & Permanent Solution Core Team Members:

The example below refers to a product focused root cause analysis team.

Typical Product Core Team (SME's)

- Design, Analysis
- Manufacturing
- External Consultants
- Suppliers
- Customer Support Individuals

Typical Peripheral (Non-Core) Include:

- Purchasing
- Sales & Marketing
- Business Development
- Admin

Step 2 – Separating Fact from Conjecture - The Is/Is Not Matrix

There is always a limited amount of critical information available to teams working on difficult or chronic problems. Separating fact from conjecture must always be done at the start of the process to provide a solid foundation of confirmed knowledge to support the root cause hypotheses development activities. Where missing information is identified, a plan must be constructed to acquire it.

Is / Is Not Matrix

The Is / Is Not matrix is a tool used to document various scenarios where the problem occurred but also and equally importantly, where the problem did not occur but logically could have. If one is able to determine the differences (physical or otherwise) between those two scenarios, therein lies a critical piece of data to help further the understanding of the actual root cause.

The Is / Is Not matrix is one of the most powerful tools in the problem resolution process toolset. Identifying a single example where the problem did and did not occur can significantly accelerate the root cause identification process. Examining the differences between these two scenarios can yield significant root cause insight. Creating this matrix is instrumental in aligning the knowledge of the team by providing information into available and missing data, ultimately separating fact from conjecture. It establishes a robust platform on which to launch the hypotheses development activities.

Example Using Scenario 1 - "Visible Vehicle Smoke" problem (ref. chapter 12)

The Is / Is Not matrix illustrated below captures both available and missing information about the problem to support the development of the root cause hypotheses activities. It aligns the team on the facts but also identifies missing information.

Illustrative example of a typical Is / Is Not Matrix

No.	IS	IS NOT	Key Differences	Actions
1	Customer X	Customer Y (Same Vehicle)	- Different driving habits - Different geographical location -Different vehicle mileages	-Gather data on key differences
2	White Smoke	Black Smoke	- White smoke typically indicative of excessive fuel or water vapor. Black smoke is typically indicative of oil.	- Analyze smoke sample to verify constituents
3	Low Engine Speed (Idling)	High Engine Speed	- Different engine operating parameters. Different engine calibration. - Different component clearances - Different crankcase pressures	- Identify key parameter differences
4	Cold Engine	Hot Engine (even at low RPMs)	- Different fueling strategies - Different breather flowrates and gas temperatures -Different oil viscosities	- Gather data and confirm
5	Car X	Car Y	- Different ratings of the same base engine. - Different breather tube locations - Different calibrations	- Develop and confirm list of all key differences
6	Cars built after May 2012	Cars built before 2012	- Minor engine calibration differences	- Confirm all key differences (hardware and software)
7	Low Mileage	Unknown	Unknown	Gather Data
8	High Mileage	Unknown	Unknown	Gather Data

The Is / Is Not matrix maintains a "live" status throughout the problem resolution project and is continually updated as new, factual data becomes available. The information in this matrix fuels the root cause hypothesis generation process. As soon as definitive scenarios exist where the problem did and did not occur but logically could have, the core team begins to interrogate each scenario to gain a thorough understanding of the specific key differences in an effort to develop insight into potential root causes.

Step 3 – Root Cause Hypotheses Development

Fuelled by the data generated by the Is / Is Not matrix, the core team is now equipped to commence the development of an extensive list of root cause hypotheses. The most effective method of capturing failure hypotheses is through a traditional brainstorming workshop supported by a core team of subject matter experts in a similar fashion to the interim solution workshop.

Cause and Effect Diagram

A preferred tool used to capture, prioritize and manage various hypotheses generated during a root cause brainstorming exercise is commonly referred to as a cause & effect diagram. This tool is based on an Ishikawa diagram originally developed in 1968 by Kaoru Ishikawa. The traditional fishbone format of the Ishikawa Diagram can sometimes limit the levels to which one can develop the root cause into its first principle constituents which in some cases makes the cause and effect diagram a preferred solution.

There are several software packages readily available to help facilitate the creation of cause and effect diagrams. However, although specialty programs exist, traditional spreadsheet software with integrated graphics which include linkage options is adequate. When complete, the cause and effect diagram must contain an exhaustive list of potential root cause hypotheses with logical flows. The team must spend sufficient time on this process step to ensure that all hypotheses have been adequately captured and are logically feasible. The graphical layout of a cause and effect diagram is instrumental in mapping the logic of each hypothesis to assist in this evaluation. This document remains live throughout the project and hypotheses prioritization is likely to continually change as new data becomes available. The cause and effect diagram can be customized as needed.

Constructing a Cause & Effect Diagram

Step 1: Brainstorming and Hypotheses Capturing

- The development of a cause and effect diagram starts with an extensive brainstorming session supported by subject matter experts and any other individuals equipped to provide problem insight.

- All hypotheses, irrespective of radical they may appear at the time of the workshop must be captured. Ranking will manage relative occurrence probabilities.

- It is important for the team generating the hypotheses to have exposure to the Is / Is Not Material to assist in prioritizing or discounting hypotheses as they are generated.

- For the initial workshops, the focus should be on the capturing of hypotheses. Processing including prioritization of the hypotheses can happen later in the process. The objective of the brainstorming session is the capturing of all ideas such that the team is satisfied that the root cause has been captured but not necessarily confirmed.

The Structure of the Cause & Effect Diagram:

- The problem is placed at the left-hand side of the diagram (Level 1)

- Each hypothesis is graphically represented by generating a granular logic progression from right to left. These various levels allow the team to verify the logic of each root cause hypothesis. This is very helpful especially at the prioritization stage.

- There are no limits to the number of levels generated. Each problem and facilitator will have unique needs and the tool can be modified to meet these.

Example Using Scenario 1 - "Visible Vehicle Smoke" problem (ref. chapter 12)

Cause and Effect Diagram Example

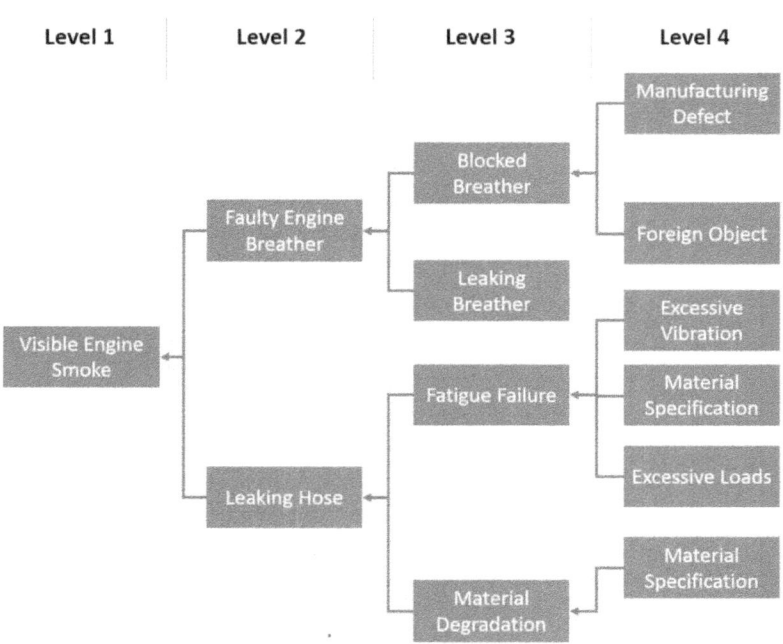

Step 2: Hypotheses Processing

- After completion of the cause & effect diagram, it is then necessary to rank each hypothesis relative to the probability of occurrence as agreed by the collective team. Each hypothesis is assigned a number that describes this ranking priority.

Prioritized Cause & Effect Diagram

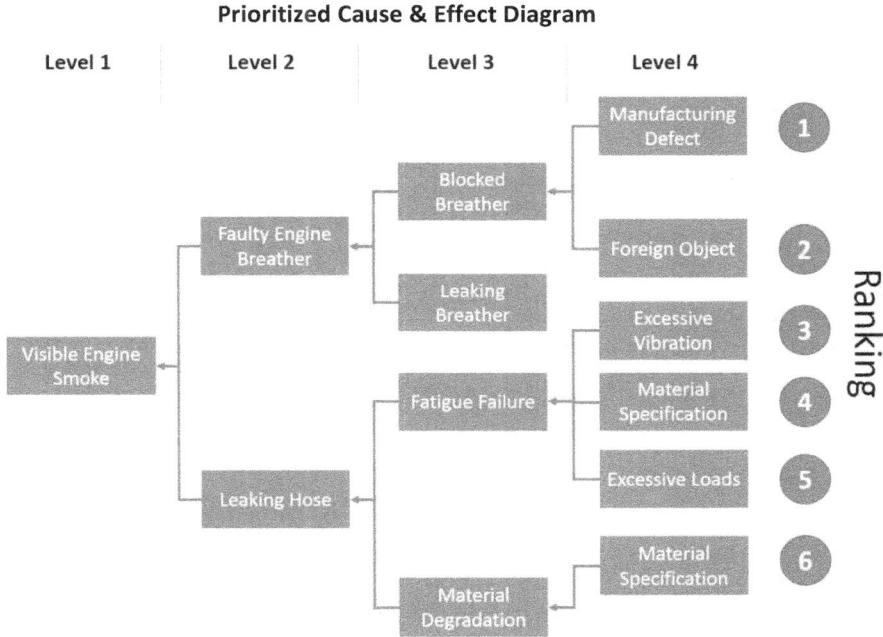

- The top 5 hypotheses are usually transferred to a worksheet for further processing. This additional processing includes:

    - Detailed description of each of the top 5 root cause hypotheses enabling anyone to clearly understand the logic behind the hypothesis.

    - Validation methodology recommended to prove or disprove the hypothesis. This can be a combination of the testing, analysis etc....

- Action list with task assignees and dates. This is particularly important to ensure that hypothesis has a clear plan with associated timing expectations for results.

Illustrative Example – Hypothesis Processing

No.	Hypothesis	Validation Method	Actions / Status
1	*Capture the prioritized hypothesis including a very detailed description in this cell.*	*The method of validation can range from analysis to physical testing. It can include the construction of scaled prototypes*	*Capturing ownership of the task of validation with a individual responsible is key to driving results*
2	*Second prioritized hypothesis*	*Second validation activity*	*Names of individuals with dates and responsibility*

- The number of hypotheses being analyzed in parallel is a function of problem severity and available project resources. Typically, 3 root cause hypotheses are addressed in parallel to avoid excessive resource dilution. Once the team completes the analysis and verification, they move onto the next highest priority item to validate assuming the root cause has not been identified.

Step 3: Hypotheses Reprioritization

As results are generated from the hypotheses prove-out activities, both the Is/Is Not and cause & effect documents are continually updated with new data. In the case of the Is / Is Not document, missing data is populated, and existing data verified or amended. In the case of the cause

& effect diagram, hypotheses that have proven false are de-ranked and the collective team adds new hypotheses to the prioritized top 5 list

Step 4 – Hypotheses Validation

The criteria that determines successful root cause identification is the ability to repeatedly turn on and off the problem under controlled conditions. This can be extremely difficult and time intensive to accomplish; it is however a mandatory step than must be accomplished to prove recurrence will not occur.

A common pitfall for these programs is the premature declaration of victory without compliance to this critical step.

Step 5 – Permanent Solution Development & Roll Out

Following the identification and verification of root cause, the team must then develop the most appropriate solution that permanently eliminates root cause.

Permanent Solution Generation Steps:

- Subject Matter Expert brainstorming to identify all potential options
- Reconciliation of proposed ideas with functional requirements and identification of any deficiencies
- Creation of a Pugh analysis to compare and prioritize solution options
    - o This includes items such as cost models

- Development of an optimized validation plan to minimize costs and maximize speed to market

Using traditional product development methodologies, the desired solution is then validated using a combination of analysis and hardware testing both in the laboratory and potentially the field.

Chapter 14 - Preventing Recurrence

The task of problem recurrence prevention is often neglected by most organizations after a problem has been resolved irrespective of the severity. The euphoric and exhausted problem resolution team usually has a backlog of work from their regular job to catch up on.

Organizations most susceptible to problem recurrence are companies where significant attrition occurs resulting in the permanent loss of knowledge, or companies weak in updating documentation such as product design guidelines.

The process for preventing knowledge loss and subsequent recurrence is the capturing of lessons learned immediately following project completion. Using this data, company procedures and policies should then be updated to safeguard against future recurrence of similar problems.

Process for Recurrence Prevention:

- Brainstorming workshop immediately after the core problem has been resolved
- Addressing a revised problem statement "What organizationally went wrong to cause the problem?"

- Updating company operating procedures and product design manuals to automatically detect and prevent future recurrence

After having worked in multiple roles for multiple major global organizations throughout my career, the process described above has always yielded the highest level of success time and time again irrespective of industry or product type.

About the Author

Paul Jones started his career working as a successful product Design Engineer in the UK. Paul then moved to the US to work at a global technical consulting firm eventually transitioning from technical to management consulting. In this role he led numerous cost reduction and problem resolution programs for various high-profile global organizations in a variety of industries ranging from automotive to alternative energy start-ups.

Paul has held numerous roles throughout his career from Engineering Manager, Director of Cost Management, Director of Engineering, VP Supply Chain and Plant Manager.

Paul holds numerous design patents and continues to support clients in their endeavors to produce highly competitive, low cost, high value solutions. Paul currently operates a consulting and product innovation company Solexpro LLC based on Austin, TX (www.solexprollc.com).